The Stone
of the Philosophers

By
Arthur Edward Waite

ISBN: 978-1-63118-509-0

Esoteric Classics

Other Books in this Series and Related Titles

Aurora of the Philosophers by Paracelsus (978-1-63118-507-6)

On the Philadelphian Gold by Philochrysus &c (978-1-63118-511-3)

The Magician's Heavenly Chaos by Thomas Vaughan (978-1-63118-500-7)

Paracelsus, the Four Elements and Their Spirits by M P Hall (978-1-63118-400-0)

Alchemy in the Nineteenth Century by Helena P. Blavatsky (978-1-63118-446-8)

Cloud Upon the Sanctuary by Waite & K Eckartshausen (978-1-63118-438-3)

The Rosicrucian Chemical Marriage by Christian Rosenkreuz (978-1-63118-458-1)

The Golden Verses of Pythagoras: Five Translations (978-1-63118-479-6)

The Hymns of Hermes by G. R. S. Mead (978-1-63118-405-5)

The Devil in Love by Jacques Cazotte (978–1–63118–499–4)

On the Cave of the Nymphs in the Odyssey by Thomas Taylor (978-1-63118-505-2)

Plato and Platonism and Related Esoteric Essays by various (978-1-63118-432-1)

Clairvoyance and Psychic Abilities by A Besant &c (978-1-63118-403-1)

The Book of Wisdom of Solomon by King Solomon (978-1-63118-502-1)

A Collection of Early Writings on Astral Travel (978-1-63118-477-2)

Rosicrucian Rules, Secret Signs, Codes and Symbols by various (978-1-63118-488-8)

The Sepher Yetzirah and the Qabalah by M P Hall (978-1-63118-481-9)

Arcane Formulas or Mental Alchemy by W W Atkinson (978-1-63118-459-8)

The Machinery of the Mind by Dion Fortune (978-1-63118-451-2)

Brothers & Builders by Joseph Fort Newton (978-1-63118-506-9)

The Leadbeater Reader: A Selection of Occult Essays (978-1-63118-483-3)

Audio versions are also available on Audible, Amazon and Apple

Other Books in this Series and Related Titles

Atlantis, the Gods of Antiquity and the Myth of the Dying God (978–1–63118–498–7)

The Mysteries of Freemasonry & the Druids by M P Hall &c (978-1-63118-444-4)

Prashna Upanishad and Commentary by Charles Johnston (978-1-63118-494-9)

The Kabbalah of Masonry & Related Writings by E Levi &c (978-1-63118-453-6)

The Legend of the Holy Grail and its Connection with Templars and Freemasons
by A E Waite (978-1-63118-462-8)

The First and Second Gospels of the Infancy of Jesus Christ
by Thomas and James (978-1-63118-415-4)

The Secrets of Enoch by Enoch (978-1-63118-449-9)

Brothers & Builders by Joseph Fort Newton (978-1-63118-506-9)

Magical Essays and Instructions by Florence Farr (978-1-63118-418-5)

Masonic and Rosicrucian History by M P Hall & H Voorhis (978-1-63118-486-4)

History and Teachings of the Rosicrucians by W W Westcott &c (978-1-63118-487-1)

The Smoky God or A Voyage to the Inner World by Emerson (978-1-63118-423-9)

The Janeites, The Man Who Would Be King and Other Stories of Freemasonry
by Rudyard Kipling (978–1–63118–480–2)

Gnosis of the Mind by G. R. S. Mead (978-1-63118-408-6)

The Master Mason's Handbook by J S M Ward (978-1-63118-474-1)

The Feminine Occult by various authors (978-1-63118-711-7)

The Leadbeater Reader: A Selection of Occult Essays (978-1-63118-483-3)

The Human Aura: Astral Colors and Thought Forms (978-1-63118-419-2)

The Path of Light: A Manual of Maha-Yana Buddhism (978-1-63118-471-0)

The Hymn of Jesus by G. R. S. Mead (978-1-63118-492-5)

Audio versions are also available on Audible, Amazon and Apple

Table of Contents

Introduction...7

Preface...9

Chapter I: *The Introduction*...11

Chapter II: *Of the Vegetable Tincture, or the Process called the Lesser Circulation*...12

Chapter III: *Of the Uses of the Vegetable Tinctures, with some general remarks on their great efficacy in medicine*...15

Chapter IV: *Of the Metallic Tincture*...21

Chapter V: *Of the Second Matter, or Seed in Metals*...28

Chapter VI: *Of the Dissolution and Extraction of the Seed in Metals*...35

Chapter VII: *Of the Separation and Further Treatment of our Philosophical Seed*...39

Chapter VIII: *Of the Union or Mystical Marriage in the Philosophical Process*...41

Chapter IX: *Of the Further Treatment and Ripening of our Seed*...44

Chapter X: *Of the Further Process to the Ripening of our Noble Seed*...46

Chapter XI: *A Further Description of the Process*...48

Chapter XII: *Of the Stone and its Uses*...49

Chapter XIII: *Of the Transmutation*...50

INTRODUCTION

The word "esoteric" can be difficult to define. Esotericism in general can be seen less as a system of beliefs and more as a category, which encompasses numerous, different systems of beliefs. It's a bit of juxtaposition, since the word "esoteric" indicates something that few people know about, while the term itself broadly covers numerous philosophies, practices, areas of study and belief systems.

In a greater sense, Esotericism acts as a storehouse for secret knowledge, which is often considered ancient (*by tradition, if not by fact*), passed down from generation to generation, in private. At various times in history, simply possessing the knowledge of some of these subjects, was considered illegal and a jailable offence, if discovered. This usually included such general topics as Alchemy, Pharmacology, Qabalah, Hermeticism, Occultism, Ceremonial Magic, Astrology, Divination, Rosicrucianism and so on. Collectively, these areas of study were often referred to as the esoteric sciences.

Sometimes, the outer garment of a subject isn't esoteric, while what is hidden beneath it, is. As an example, Freemasonry isn't necessarily esoteric by nature (at *least not anymore*), but certain signs, passwords and handshakes given to the candidate during their initiation, are in fact, esoteric, in the sense that they are hidden from the general public.

Today, in the twenty-first century, such topics are readily available at bookstores across the country, and numerous mainsteam publishers offer beginners guides and coffee-table volumes on many of these subjects, intended for mass appeal. Books like *"The Secret"* have turned previously arcane topics into household knowledge. All that being the case, however, it isn't to say that there still aren't buried secrets to uncover, ancient wisdom being ignored and forgotten mysteries to be explored. In fact, it is often that we are only able to further our own studies by standing on the shoulders of these disappearing giants.

Lamp of Trismegistus is doing its part to help preserve humanity's esoteric history by making some of these classics available to those students who are seeking to unearth the knowledge of these ancient colossi.

So, be sure to check other titles from our *Esoteric Classics* series, as well as our *Occult Fiction, Theosophical Classics, Foundations of Freemasonry Series, Supernatural Fiction, Paranormal Research Series, Studies in Buddhism* and our *Christian Apocrypha Series*. You can also download the audio versions of most of these titles from Amazon, Apple or Audible, for learning on the go.

PREFACE

If there had been any English publication upon this curious and momentous subject, easy to be met with, that deserved regard, the public had not been troubled with this. The operations herein described are all within the compass of Nature; they are laid down in plain language, and the reasoning upon them is suited to a common apprehension, where there is a chemical turn of mind. Anyone inclining to these studies, if poor, will do well to mind his proper business, without attempting the Philosophical Work, as the necessary apparatus must require more expense and time than he can spare; but such as are of ability may well undertake it, both as a recreation and useful employment, in which an ingenious laborer may be retained as an assistant for the manual operations, at such a daily allowance as may be proportioned to his labor and sufficient for a subsistence. No more can be expected by a man who is modest and pious: one that is vicious can never be depended upon in a work of consequence like this, where patience is a main requisite, together with a punctilious veracity in reciting every variation of the matter during a tedious process from seven to nine months.

Whoever will therefore undertake this process must needs have an assistant; and, we again repeat it, such an one whose fidelity, above all things, may be safely relied upon; true, faithful, and religious; being, like his employer, acute to investigate the phenomena of Nature, especially in chemical processes.

Those who are accustomed to treat this science with contempt may doubtless ridicule anything written expressly upon it without examining what is advanced in its support, the title only of a book being of a sufficient reason with many for their disregarding the contents. We shall leave such superficial people in quiet possession of that unhappy self-sufficiency they have acquired, and rather apologize for the plainness with which this process is delivered to those possessors of it, if any, and yet alive, who may be displeased with our public spirit in communicating what has so long been considered as a sacred deposition with a few Philosophers.

CHAPTER I

The Introduction

Because many have written of the Philosopher's Stone without any knowledge of the art; and the few books extent, written by our learned predecessors and true masters hereupon, are either lost or concealed in the collections of such (*however despised*) as are lovers and seekers of natural secrets, we have taken a resolution to communicate our knowledge in this matter, to the intent that those who are convinced the Philosophical Work is no fiction, but grounded in the possibility of Nature, may be faithfully directed in their studies, and have an undoubted criterion to distinguish between such authors as are genuine sons of science and those who are spurious, as writing by hearsay only.

We shall not on this occasion give a summary of their names who are undoubted masters in the art, but shall take occasion to introduce them, as it may be necessary, in the following chapters; and as their sense is often concealed under a studied ambiguity of expression, we shall, out of the gift which the Almighty hath dispensed to us, declare plainly, and without any reserve, the first matter of the Philosopher's Stone, the manner of proceeding through the whole process, both in the Vegetable and Metallic Tinctures, beginning with the Vegetable process first, as the most easy and simple, yet well worthy the attention of all ingenious persons, particularly the practical chemists and preparers of medicines.

CHAPTER II

Of the Vegetable Tincture, or the Process called the Lesser Circulation

Very few of the true philosophers have touched upon this subject, for it seemed trifling in respect to the great work, as the process in metals is generally termed; but there is a modern publication in English, a small thin duodecimo, without any author's name, having for its title: Aphorismi, seu Circulus majus et Circulus minus, wherein the whole process is plainly laid down.

This book is written by an undoubted master in the art; and no treatise, ancient or modern, is so explicit in the directions for conducting the great work. The directions are very short, but much to the purpose, provided the reader has an idea what part of the work is alluded to. The author, agreeable to his title, delivers his doctrine by way of aphorisms. But to return from this digression.

We proposed in this chapter to lay open the vegetable process, as a clue to the more important work in the mineral kingdom. A certain person, who is now living, and advertises balsam of honey, tincture of sage, etc, has turned his studies this way; and from his great abilities as a professed physician and botanist, has convinced all unprejudiced persons that noble tinctures may be extracted from vegetables. We hope this gentleman will not despise our free communication, both to him and the public, if we show the insufficiency of his method, though it is ingenious, while we establish the rationale of ours on the never-failing ground of truth and philosophy.

He observes, with a precision which can only result from numerous trials, that different herbs impart their tinctures in such proportions of alcohol as he has found out. It is allowed that the volatile spirit and balsamic sulphur are thus extracted; but there are the essential, or fixed, salt and sulphur of the herb yet left in the process. These require another management to extract, which he is either ignorant of, or is so disingenuous as to conceal from the public; but that so noble a secret may lie open to all for a general advantage, here follows a plain account of the vegetable work.

Take any herb which is potent in medicine, and either extract the tincture with spirit of wine, or distil in the common way; reserve the distilled water, or tincture, when separated from the feces, for use. Then take the feces, or Caput Mortuum, and calcine it to a calx. Grind this to powder.

That done, take the water, or tincture, and mix them together; distil again, and calcine, forcing the moisture over by a retort, in a wary process, calcining and cohobating the spirit on the salt till it attains a perfect whiteness and oily nature, like the finest alkali, commonly called Flemish.

As your salt requires it in the process, have in readiness more of the extracted tincture, or distilled spirit, that you may not work it, viz., the salt, too dry; and yet proceed cautiously, not adding too much of the moisture, so that the dealbating, or whitening, may keep visibly heightening at every repetition of the process. Frequent experiments may enable you to push it on to a redness, but a fine yellow is the best of all; for the process tends, in its perfection at this period, to a state of dryness, and must be managed with a strong fire. By following these directions, you have here the two tinctures in the Vegetable Kingdom, answering to the white and red tinctures in the mineral.

CHAPTER III

Of the Uses of the Vegetable Tinctures, with some general remarks on their great efficacy in medicine

You have, by carefully following our directions above, procured the tinctures, white or yellow, in the Vegetable Kingdom. The yellow is more efficacious if the work is well performed; either of them, by being exposed in the air, will soon run into a thick, essential oil, smelling very strong of the plant, and the virtues of any quantity may be concentrated by often repeating the circulation. But you have no need of this, unless for curiosity, there being in your tinctures a real permanent power to extract the essential virtues of any herb you may require on immersion only, where the essential salt and volatile spirit, together with the sulphureous oil, are all conjoined, floating on the top of your tincture, and the terrestrial feces precipitated to the bottom; not as in distillation, or extraction of the tincture with alcohol, while the stalk and texture of the plant are entire; no, this Vegetable Tincture devours the whole substance of the plant, and precipitates only the earthy particles acquired in its vegetation, which no degree of calcination could push to an alkali, without its essential salt.

Such is the virtue of our Vegetable Tincture; and if the operation be never so often repeated with different herbs, it loses nothing of its virtue, or quantity or quality, casting up the virtues of whatever herb is immersed, and precipitating the earth as before when both are easily separated and the medicine preserved for use.

Let a medicine, thus prepared, be examined, and the principles by which it is extracted, with the general methods of preparation; if the distilled water for instance, of any aromatical or balsamic herb, be took, common experience will convince us that nothing but its volatile parts come over the head; but take the Caput Mortuum, and it will calcine after this process, and afford an alkali, which proves itself to be an essential salt by its pungency, and will, in the air, run to an oil, which is its essential sulphur. If you take the tincture extracted with alcohol, it is the same, only the more resinous parts of some herbs may enrich the extract, and the volatile sulphur giving the color and scent, be retained, which escapes in distillation; but the potent virtue or soul of the herb, if we may be allowed the expression, goes to the dunghill. It is the same if the expressed juice of the herb is used; and if taken in powder, or substance, as it is sometimes prescribed, but little of its virtue, beyond its nourishing quality, can be communicated to the patient, except as a bitter or a vermifuge, in which cases, perhaps, it is best by way of infusion.

Let none despise the operation above laid down, because it is not to be found in the ordinary books of chemistry; but consider the possibility of Nature, who brings about wonderful effects by the most simple causes: neither let any imagine this process so easy as to perform it without some trials, patiently attending to her operations and endeavoring to account for any deficiency in the course of his work. For this reason it will be proper that the artist forms to himself an idea what the intention is to procure, how far Nature has prepared his matter to work upon, in what state she has left it, and how far it may be exalted above the ordinary point of virtue, which it could attain in the crude air, and this by the Philosophic Art assisting Nature, as a handmaid, with an administration of due heat, which is nutritive and not corrosive.

A recapitulation of the foregoing process, with some remarks on the different stages, will be sufficient here to explain our meaning above, and prepare the reader for what follows concerning the metallic tincture, or Stone of the Philosophers.

The virtues of herbs and simples are confessedly great and manifold; among these, some are poisonous and narcotic, yet of great use in medicine; none of them but want some preparation or correction. Now the common ways of doing this are defective; neither preserving the virtue entire, nor furnishing any menstruum capable of doing it with expedition and certainty. Alcohol, as was before observed, will extract a tincture and distillation a spirit. We reject neither of these methods in our work, as they are useful to decompound the subject; but we are not content with a part of its virtues.

To speak philosophically, we would have its soul, which is in its Essential Salt, and its spirit, which is in the Inflammable Sulphur. The body in which these resided we are not concerned for; it is mere earth, and must return from whence it came: whereas the soul and spirit are paradisiacal, if the artist can free them from their earthy prison without loss; but this can only be done by death. Understand us aright. Philosophically speaking, no more is meant than decomposition of the subject into its first principles, as the uniting them more permanently with an increase of virtue is most emphatically called a resurrection and regeneration. Now this decompounding is to be done with judgment, so as not to corrode or destroy, but divide the matter into its integral parts. At this period of the work the artist will consider what is further intended, keeping Nature in view, who, if she is properly assisted in her operations, produces from the dissolution of any subject something more excellent, as in a grain of corn, or any vegetable seed, which by cultivation may be pushed to a surprising produce; but then it must die first, as our Blessed Saviour very emphatically observes: and let this saying dwell upon the artist's imagination, that he may know what he generally intends; for the whole philosophical work, both in vegetables and minerals, is only a mortifying of the subject, and reviving it again to a more excellent life.

Now if the intention in the foregoing process was to increase simply any vegetable in its kind, the destruction and revivification must follow the ordinary course of vegetation by the medium of seed; and Nature can only be assisted by fertilizing the soil, together with a proper distribution of heat and moisture. Yet there are not wanting authors, and particularly Paracelsus, who boldly describe processes wherein the vital quality of the seed has been destroyed by calcination, and yet brought to life again at the pleasure of an artist. Such reveries are a scandal to philosophy, and a snare to the superficial reader, who is generally more struck with impossibilities, roundly asserted, than the modesty of true artists. These confess their operations are within the bounds of Nature, whose limits they cannot surpass.

The reader, then, will consider that our intention here is not to increase the seminal quality, but to concenter, in a little compass, the medicinal virtues of a herb. Nature is desirous of this in all her productions, but can only rise to such a point of perfection, in her ordinary course, through the crudity of the air and fixing power of the elements. Now if we take the vegetables at that point of perfection to which she has pushed them, and farther assist her in decompounding, purifying, uniting, and reviving the subject, we obtain, what she could not otherwise produce, a real permanent tincture, the quintessence, as it is called, or such a harmonious mixture of the four elementary qualities as constitutes a fifth, from thenceforth indissoluble, and not to be debased with any impurity.

But the virtue of this Vegetable Tincture is capable of improvement ad infinitum, in its own kind, by adding more of its spirit or extracted tincture, and repeating the circulation, which is every time more speedily finished, as there is a magnetical quality in the fixed salt, and essential oil, which assimilates to itself all the real virtues of what is added, only rejecting the feculent, earthy qualities; so that in a grain of the tincture much virtue may be concentered, not at all corrosive or ardent, but friendly to the animal life, and most powerful as a medicine for disorders which the herb is appropriated to cure. Nay, something of this nature was still sought for by the distillers of ardent spirits, when phlegm has been drawn away from the volatile sulphur, till it becomes proof spirit, as it is termed, which will burn dry, a plain indication that it contained nothing essential in it from the subject out of which it was extracted: for that which is essential cannot be destroyed by the fire, but is reddened to an alkaline salt, having in its center an Incombustible Sulphur, which, on exposing to the air, manifests itself both to the sight and touch. Now, if this Salt and Sulphur are purified, and the distilled spirit, or extracted tincture, added, Nature finds a subject wherein she can carry her operations to the highest limit, if an artist furnishes her with proper vessels, and a degree of heat suitable to her intentions.

CHAPTER IV

Of the Metallic Tincture

When we undertook a description of the vegetable process, it was chiefly with a view to familiarize the reader to a general idea of the Philosophic Work in metals, as both proceed upon the same principles, only the mercuries of metals are more difficult to extract, and stronger degrees of heat are required, as well as more of the artist's time and patience; neither can he succeed in the operation without frequent trials, and a constant consideration within his mind as to what is within the possibility of Nature.

For this purpose it is necessary to know the composition of metals, that he may know how to decompound and reduce them to their first principles, which is treated of very mysteriously by the philosophers, and purposely concealed, as the right key to unlock all the secrets of Nature. We shall be more explicit on this head, for the time draws near when, as Sendivogius has observed, the confection of the Stone will be discovered as plainly as the making of cheese from rennet. But we warn the reader not to imitate Midas in the fable, by seeking the noble tincture in metals out of covetousness; for the true wise men seek only a medicine for human infirmities, and esteem gold but as it furnishes them with the means of independence and the exercise of universal beneficence. They communicate their talents, without vain glory or ostentation, to such as are worthy searchers of Nature, but concealing their names as much as possible, while living, as well as their knowledge of the mystery from the world.

We shall herein follow their example, and yet write more plainly of the Metallic Process than any of them has hitherto done, knowing that the providence of the Most High will effectually guard this Arcanum from falling into the hands of covetous gold seekers and knavish pretenders to the Art of Transmutation; because the first sort of men will, from their impatience, soon leave the simplicity of Nature for processes of more subtlety invented by the latter, and adapted to such avaricious views as the other have formed, who, judging of things by their own griping dispositions, know not the noble liberality of Nature, but imagine some gold must be advanced before she will replenish their heaps. This is well foreseen by those smoke sellers, who receive what they can catch, as if they were her proper agents; and, having no conscience to put a stop to their imposition, the deception is kept up till all vanishes in smoke.

Let it be observed, then, that all who have written on the art, from undoubted principles, assert that the genuine process is not expensive; time and fuel, with manual labour, being all allowed for. Besides, the matter to be wrought upon is easy to procure by the consent of all. A small quantity of gold and silver is, indeed, necessary when the stone is made, as a medium for its tinging either in the white or red tinctures, which such pretenders have urged from books of philosophers as a plausible pretense to rob the avaricious both of their time and money; but their pretenses are so gross that none can be sufferers in this respect, if they have not justly deserved it.

The reader may then rest assured that this process is not expensive, and reject all authors or practitioners who advance anything contrary to this established verity, remembering the simplicity of Nature in her operations, observing her frugal method in the production, and consummate wisdom in the dissolution of things; always endeavoring at something perfect in a new production. And because we are here proposing to help her in a metallic process, as before in the vegetable, let us consider a little how she forms the metals, in what state she has left them, and what need there is of the artist's skill to assist her in pushing them to that degree of perfection they are capable of attaining.

All true philosophers agree that the First Matter of metals is a moist vapor, raised by the action of the central fire in the bowels of the earth, which, circulating through its pores, meets with the crude air, and is coagulated by it into an unctuous water, adhering to the earth, which serves it for a receptacle, where it is joined to a sulphur more or less pure, and a salt more or less fixing, which it attracts from the air, and, receiving a certain degree of concoction from the central and solar heat, is formed into stones and rocks, minerals, and metals. These were all formed of the same moist vapor originally, but are thus varied from the different impregnations of the sperm, the quality of salt and sulphur with which it is fixed, and the purity of the earth which serves it for a matrix; for whatever portion of this moist vapor is taking along its impurities, is soon deprived of heat, both solar and central, and the grosser parts, forming a mucilaginous substance, furnish the matter of common rocks and stones. But when this moist vapor is sublimed, very slowly, through a fine earth, not partaking of a sulphureous unctuously, pebbles are formed; for the sperm of these beautiful, variegated stones, with marbles, alabasters, etc., separates this depurated vapor, both for their first formation and continual growth. Gems are in like manner formed of this moist vapor when it meets with pure salt water, with which it is fixed in a cold place. But if it is sublimed leisurely through places which are hot and pure, where the fatness of sulphur adheres to it, this vapor, which the philosophers call their Mercury, is joined to that fatness and becomes an unctuous matter, which coming afterwards to other places, cleansed by the afore-named vapors, where the earth is subtle, pure, and moist, fills the pores of it, and so gold is made.

But if the unctuous matter comes into places cold and impure, lead, or Saturn, is produced; if the earth be cold and pure, mixed with sulphur, the result is copper. Silver also is formed of this vapor, where it abounds in purity, but mixed with a laser degree of sulphur and not sufficiently concocted. In tin, or Jupiter, as it is called, it abounds, but in less purity. In Mars, or iron, it is in a lesser proportion impure, and mixed with an adjust sulphur.

Hence it appears that the First Matter of metals is one thing, and not many, homogeneous, but altered by the diversity of places and sulphurs with which it is combined. The philosophers frequently describe this matter.

Sendivogius calls it heavenly water, not wetting the hands; not vulgar, but almost like rain water. When Hermes calls it a bird without wings, figuring thereby its vaporous nature, is it well described. When he calls the sun its father and the moon its mother, he signifies that it is produced by the action of heat upon moisture. When he says the wind carries it in its belly, he only means that the air is its receptacle. When he affirms that which is inferior is like that which is superior, he teaches that the same vapor on the surface of the earth furnishes the matter of rain and dew, wherewith all things are nourished in the vegetable and animal kingdoms. This now is what the philosophers call their Mercury and affirm it to be found in all things, as it is in fact. This makes some suppose it to be in the human body, others in the dunghill, which has often bewildered such as are fond of philosophical subtleties, and fly from one thing to another, without any fixed theory about what they would seek, expecting to find in the Vegetable or Animal Kingdoms the utmost perfection of the Mineral. To this mistake of theirs, without doubt, the philosophers have contributed with an intention of hiding their First Matter from the unworthy; in which they were, perhaps, more cautious than is necessary, for Sendivogius declares that occasionally, in discourse, he had intimated the art plainly word by word to some who accounted themselves very accurate philosophers; but they conceived such subtle notions, far beyond the simplicity of Nature, that they could not, to any purpose, understand his meaning. Wherefore, he professes little fear of its being discovered but to those who have it according to the good pleasure and providence of the Most High.

This benevolent disposition has induced him to declare more openly the First Matter, and fix the artist in his search of it to the mineral kingdom; for, quoting Albertus Magnus, who wrote that, in his time, grains of gold were found betwixt the teeth of a dead man in his grave, he observes that Albertus could not account for this miracle, but judged it to be by reason of the mineral virtue in man, being confirmed by that saying of Morien: "And this matter, O King, is extracted from thee." But this is erroneous, for Morien understood those things philosophically, the mineral virtue residing in its own kingdom, distinct from the animal.

It is true, indeed, in the animal kingdom mercury, or humidity, is as the matter, and sulphur, or marrow in the bones, as the virtue; but the animal is not mineral, and vice versa. If the virtue of the animal sulphur were not in man, the blood, or mercury, could not be coagulated into flesh and bones; so if there were not a vegetable sulphur in the vegetable kingdom, it could not coagulate water, or the vegetable mercury, into herbs, etc. The same is to be understood in the mineral kingdom.

These three kingdoms do not, indeed, differ in their virtue, nor the three sulphurs, as every sulphur has a power to coagulate its own mercury; and every mercury has a power of being coagulated by its own proper sulphur, and by no other which is a stranger to it.

Now the reason why gold was found betwixt the teeth of a dead man is this: because in his lifetime mercury had been administered to him, either by unction, turbid, or some other way; and it is the nature of this metal to ascend to the mouth, forming itself an outlet there, to be evacuated with the spittle. If, then, in the time of such treatment, the sick man died, the mercury, not finding an egress, remained in his mouth between his teeth, and the carcass becoming a natural matrix to ripen the mercury, it was shut up for a long time, till it was congealed into gold by its own proper sulphur, being purified by the corrosive phlegm of the man's body; but this would never have happened if mineral mercury had not been administered to him.

CHAPTER V

Of the Second Matter, or Seed in Metals

All philosophers affirm, with one consent, that metals have a seed by which they are increased, and that this seminal quality is the same in all of them; but it is perfectly ripened in gold only, where the bond of union is so fixed that it is most difficult to decompound the subject, and procure it for the Philosophical Work. But some, who were adepts in the art, have by painful processes taken gold for their male, and the mercury, which they knew how to extract from the less compacted metals, for a female: not as an easier process, but to find out the possibility of making the stone this way; and have succeeded, giving this method more openly to conceal the true confection, which is most easy and simple. We shall, therefore, set before the reader a landmark, to keep him from tripping on this difficulty, by considering what is the seed wherein the metals are increased, that the artist may be no longer at a loss where to seek for it, keeping in view the writings of our learned predecessors on this subject.

The seed of metals is what the Sons of Wisdom have called their mercury, to distinguish it from quicksilver, which it nearly resembles, being the radical moisture of metals. This, when judiciously extracted, without corrosives, or fluxing, contains in it a seminal quality whose perfect ripeness is only in gold; in the other metals it is crude, like fruits which are yet green, not being sufficiently digested by the heat of the sun and action of the elements. We observed that the radical moisture contains the seed, which is true: yet it is not the seed, but the sperm only, in which the vital principle floats, being invisible to the eye. But the mind perceives it, and in a true artist, as a central point of condensed air, wherein Nature, according to the will of God, has included the first principles of life in everything, as well animal and vegetable as mineral; for in animals the sperm may be seen, but not the included principle of impregnation: this is a concentered point, to which the sperm serves only as a vehicle, till, by the action and ferment of the matrix, the point wherein Nature has included a vital principle expands itself, and then it is perceivable in the rudiments of an animal. So in any succulent fruit (*as, for instance, in an apple*), the pulp or sperm is much more in proportion than the seed included; and even that which appears to be seed is only a finer concoction of sperm, including the vital stamina; as also in a grain of wheat the flour is only the sperm, the point of vegetation is an included air, which is kept by its sperm from the extremes of cold and heat, till it finds a proper matrix, where the husk being softened with moisture, and warmed by the heat, the surrounding sperm putrefies, making the seed, or concentered air, to expand and to burst the husk carrying along in its motion a milky substance, assimilated to itself from the putrefied sperm. This the condensing quality of the air includes in a film and hardens into a germ, all according to the purpose of Nature.

"If this whole process of Nature, most wonderful in her operations, was not constantly repeated before our eyes, the simple process of vegetation would be equally problematical with that of the philosophers; yet how can the metals increase, nay, how can anything be multiplied without seed? The true artists never pretend to multiply metals without it, and can it be denied that Nature still follows her first appointment? She always fructifies the seed when it is put into a proper matrix. Does not she obey an ingenious artist, who knows her operations, with her possibilities, and attempts nothing beyond them? A husbandman meliorates his ground with compost, burns the weeds, and makes use of other operations. He steeps his seed in various preparations, only taking care not to destroy its vital principle; indeed, it never comes into his head to roast it, or to boil it, in which he shows more knowledge of Nature than some would-be philosophers do. Nature, like a liberal mother, rewards him with a more plentiful harvest, in proportion as he has meliorated her seed and furnished a more suitable matrix for its increase.

"The intelligent gardener goes farther; he knows how to shorten the process of vegetation, or retard it. He gathers roses, cuts salads, and pulls green peas in winter. Are the curious inclined to admire plants and fruit of other climates? He can produce them in his stoves to perfection. Nature follows his directions unconstrained, always willing to obtain her end, viz., the perfection of her offspring.

"Open your eyes here, yet studious searchers of Nature! Is she so liberal in her perishing productions, how much more in those which are permanent, and can subsist in the fire? Attend, then, to her operations; if you procure the metallic seed, and ripen that by art which she is many ages in perfecting, it cannot fail but she will regard you with an increase proportioned to the excellency of your subject.

"The reader will be apt to exclaim here: "Very fine! All this is well; but how shall the seed of metals be procured, and whence comes it that so few know how to gather it?' To this it is answered that the philosophers have hitherto industriously kept that a profound secret; some out of selfish disposition, though otherwise good men. Others, who wished only for worthy persons to whom they might impart it, could not write of it openly, because covetousness and vanity have been governing principles in the world: and, being wise men, they knew that it was not the will of the most High to inflame and cherish such odious tempers, the genuine offspring of pride and self-love, but to banish them out of the earth, wherefore they have been withheld hitherto. But we, finding no restraint on our mind in that respect, shall declare what we know: and the rather because we judge the time is come to demolish the golden calf, so long had in veneration by all ranks of men, insomuch that worth is estimated by the money a man possesses; and such is the inequality of possessions that mankind are almost reducible to the rich, who are rioting in extravagance, and the poor, who are in extreme want, smarting under the iron hand of oppression. Now the measure of inequality among the rich hastens to its limit, and the cry of the poor is come before the Lord: "Who will give them to eat till they shall be satisfied?"

Hereafter the rich shall see the vanity of their possessions when compared with the treasures communicated by this secret; for the riches it bestows are a blessing from God, and not the squeezing of oppression. Besides, its chief excellence consists in making a medicine capable of healing all diseases to which the human body is liable, and prolonging life to the utmost limits ordained by the Creator of all things.

There want not other reasons for the manifestation of the process; for skepticism has gone hand in hand with luxury and oppression, insomuch that the fundamental truths of all revealed religion are disputed. These were always held in veneration by the possessors of this art, as may be seen from what they have left upon record in their books: and, indeed, the first principles of revealed religion are demonstrated from the whole process, for the seed of metals is shown in corruption, and raised in incorruption; it is sown a natural body, and raised a spiritual body; it is known to partake of the curse which came upon the earth for man's sake, having in its composition a deadly poison, which can only be separated by regeneration in water and fire; it can, when it is thoroughly purified and exalted, immediately tinge imperfect metals and raise them to a state of perfection, being in this respect a lively emblem of that seed of the woman, the Serpent Bruiser, who, through His sufferings and death, hath entered into glory, having thenceforth power and authority to redeem, purify, and glorify all those who come unto Him as a mediator between God and mankind.

Such being our motives, we can no longer be silent concerning the seed of metals, but declare that it is contained in the ores of metals, as wheat is in the grain; and the sottish folly of alchemists has hindered them from adverting to this, so that they have always sought it in the vulgar metals, which are factitious and not a natural production, therein acting as foolishly as if a man should sow bread and expect corn from it, or from an egg which is boiled hope to produce a chicken. Nay, though the philosophers have said many times the vulgar metals are dead, not excepting gold, which passes the fire, they could never imagine a thing so simple as that the seed of metals was contained in their ores, where alone it ought to be expected; so bewildered is human ingenuity, when it leaves the beaten track of truth and Nature, to entangle itself in a multiplicity of fine-spun inventions.

The searcher of Nature will rejoice greatly in this discovery, as grounded in reason and sound philosophy, but to fools it would be in vain, should even wisdom herself cry out in the streets. Wherefore, leaving such persons to hug themselves in their own imaginary importance, we shall go on to observe that the ores of metals are our First Matter, or sperm, wherein the seed is contained, and the key of this art consists in a right dissolution of the ores into a water, which the philosophers call their mercury, or water of life, and an earthy substance, which they have denominated their sulphur.

The first is called their woman, wife, Luna, and other names, signifying that it is the feminine quality in their seed; and the other they have designated their man, husband, Sol, etc., to point out its masculine quality.

In the separation and due conjunction of these with heat, and careful management, there is generated a noble offspring, which they have for its excellency called the quintessence or a subject wherein the four elements are so completely harmonized as to produce a fifth subsisting in the fire, without waste of substance, or diminution of its virtue, wherefore they have given it the titles of Salamander, Phoenix, and Son of the Sun.

CHAPTER VI

Of the Dissolution and Extraction of the Seed in Metals

The true Sons of Science have always accounted the dissolution of metals as the master key to this art, and have been particular in giving directions concerning it, only keeping their readers in the dark as to the subject, whether ores, or factitious metals, were to be chosen: nay, when they say most to the purpose, then they make mention of metals rather than the ores, with an intention to perplex those whom they thought unworthy of the art.

Thus the author of the "Philosophical Duet," or a dialogue between the stone, gold, and mercury, says:

"By the omnipotent God, and on the salvation of my soul, I here declare to you earnest seekers, in pity to your earnest searching, the whole Philosophical Work, which is only taken from one subject and perfected in one thing. For we take this copper, and destroy it crude and gross body; we draw out its pure spirit, and after we have purified the earthy parts, we join them together, thus making a Medicine of a Poison."

It is remarkable that he avoids mentioning the ore, but calls his subject copper, which is what they call a metal of the vulgar, being indeed factitious, and not fit for the confection of our Stone, having lost its seminal quality in the fire; but in other respects it is the plainest discovery extant, and is accounted to be so by Sendivogius.

Yet the reader is not to suppose that the ore of copper is to be chosen in consequence of that assertion, as preferable to others. No, the mercury, which is the metallic seed, is attainable from all, and is easier to be extracted from lead, which is confirmed by the true adepts, advising us to seek for the noble child where it lies in a despised form, shut up under the seal of Saturn; and, indeed, let it be supposed, for an illustration of this subject, that any one would propose to make malt, he may effect his purpose in the other grains, but barley is generally chosen, because its germ is made to sprout by a less tedious process, which is to all intents and purposes what we want in the extraction of our mercury: neither are the proceeding different in both cases, if regard is had to the fixity of ores, and the ease with which barley gives forth its seminal virtue from the slight cohesion of its parts.

Let the artist remark how a maltster manages his grain by wetting, to loosen the cohesion of its parts, and leaves the rest to Nature, knowing that she will soon furnish the necessary heat for his purpose, if he does not suffer it to escape by mismanagement in his laying of his heap too thin, or raising the fermentation too high by a contrary proceeding, as it is well known actual fire may be kindled from the fermentation of vegetable juices when crude; and ripe corn, under such treatment, would soon be fit for nothing but hogs, or the dunghill. Now the intention is to raise such a fermentation only as will draw out the vegetable mercury without spoiling it, either for the earth, if it was cast there to fructify, or the kiln, if it is to be fixed at that precise point, by exhaling the Adventitious moisture, and thus preserving the whole strength of its seminal quality for the purposes of brewing, or making malt spirits.

Suppose, then, an artist would extract a mineral mercury from the ores, and chooses an ore for his subject. He can only assist Nature in the process by stirring up a central heat, which she includes in everything not already putrefied, as a root of its life, in which it is increased. The medium by which this central heat is put in motion is known to be putrefaction; but the ores of every kind are found to resist putrefaction in all known processes extant. They may, indeed, when they have been fluxed in the fire, contract a rust from the air, which is a gradual decomposition of their substance, but this is only the natural decay of a dead body, not the putrefaction of its sperm for the purposes of propagation; and we are sensible from the heat of furnaces which is required to flux the ores, and the slowness of their decay when deprived of their seminal qualities, by fluxation, that a heat which would destroy the seed in vegetables may be necessary in the first stages of putrefaction for the ores, as they will bear a red fire without being fluxed or losing anything but their sulphureous and arsenical impurities; in short, a matter in itself as much extraneous to the seed of metals, as the chaff to the wheat; wherefore, a careful separation of these by roasting, or otherwise, is deservedly reckoned among the first operations for the putrefaction of ores, and the rather because that which has been calcined, by having its pores opened, is rendered attractive, both of the air and other menstruums proper for its decomposition.

Let the artist, therefore, by fire and manual operation, separate the impure qualities from his subject, pounding, washing, and calcining, till no more blackness is communicated to his menstruum, for which pure rain water is sufficient. It will be seen on every repetition of this process, that what fouls the water is extraneous and the ore yet exists in its individual metallic nature, except it is fluxed by a too intense heat, in which case it is no longer fit for our purpose; therefore fresh ore is to be used.

The matter being thus prepared, its central fire will be awakened, if it is treated properly, according to the process for extracting quicksilver from its ores, by keeping it in a close heat, which is continued without admission of the crude air, till the radical moisture is elevated in the form of a vapor, and again condensed into a metallic water, analogous to quicksilver.

This is the true mercury of the Philosophers, and fit for all their operations in the Hermetic Art.

CHAPTER VII

Of the Separation and Further Treatment of our Philosophical Seed

The Putrefaction of our subject being thus completed, it exists under two forms; the moisture which was extracted, and the residuum, being our Philosophical Earth. The water contains its seminal virtue, and the earth is a proper receptacle, wherein it may fructify. Let the water, then, be separated and kept for use; calcine the earth, for an impurity adheres to it which can only be taken away by fire, and that, too, of the strongest degree; for here there is no danger of destroying the seminal quality, and our earth must be highly purified before it can ripen the seed. This is what Sendivogius means when he says: Burn the sulphur till it becomes Sulphur incombustible. Many lose in the preparation what is of most use in the art; for our mercury is corrected (*healed*) by the sulphur, else it would be of no use. Let, therefore, the earthy part be well calcined, and return the mercury on the calcined earth; afterwards draw it off by distillation; then calcine, cohere, and distill, repeating the process till the mercury is well corrected by the sulphur, and the sulphur is purified to a whiteness, and goes on to red, a sign of its complete purification, where you have the Philosophical Male and Female ready for conjunction.

This must now be managed with judgment, as the noble child may be yet strangled in the birth; but all things are easy to an ingenious artist, who knows the proportion of mixture required and accommodates his operations to the intention of

Nature, for which purpose we shall faithfully conduct him according to our ability.

CHAPTER VIII

Of the Union or Mystical Marriage in the Philosophical Process

The seed and its earth being thus prepared, nothing remains but a judicious conjunction of them together; for it too much moisture prevails, the philosophical egg may burst before it can go through the heat necessary for its hatching. To speak without a figure. Our subject must now be enclosed in a small glass vial, made strong enough to bear a due heat, which is to be raised gradually to the highest degree: the best form for this vessel being that of an oil flask, with a long neck; but these are much too thin in substance for this operation. In such a vessel the mixture is to be sealed hermetically, and digested so long till it is fixed into a dry concretion; but, if, as we observed, the moisture should predominate, there is great danger of the vessel bursting, with a vapor which cannot be concentered by the fixing quality in the matter. The intention is, nevertheless, to fix our subject in the heat, and so render its future destruction impossible.

On the other hand, if the dry, fixing quality of the sulphur exceeds so as not to suffer an alternate resolution of its substance into vapors, and a re- manifestation of its fixing quality, by causing the whole to subside in the bottom of the vessel till the matter again liquefies and sublimes (*which Ripley has well described*), there is danger of the whole vitrifying; and thus you shall have only glass instead of the noble tincture. To avoid these two extremes it is very proper that the purified earth be reduced by manual operation to an impalpable fineness, and then its corrected mercury must be added, incorporating both together till the earth will imbibe no more. This operation will require time, with some degree of the artist's patience; for however the humidity may seem disproportionate, on letting it rest awhile, a dryness on the surface of your matter will show that it is capable of imbibing more, so that the operation is to be repeated till it is fully saturated, which may be known from its bearing the air without any remarkable change of surface from dry to humid; or, on the contrary, if so, the conjunction is well made, which is farther confirmed if a small portion be spread upon a thin plate if iron, heated till it flows gently like wax, casting forth the moisture with heat and again absorbing it when cold, so as to return to the former consistence; but if a clamminess ensures it is a sign you have exceeded in the quantity of humidity, which must be extracted by distilling again and repeating the process till it is right.

Your sulphur and mercury being thus united, put them into a glass vial, before described, in such a quantity as to take up one-third of its contents, leaving two-thirds, including the neck, for the circulation of your matter.

Secure the neck of your vial with a temporary luting at the first, and give a gentle heat, observing whether it sublimes and fixes alternately. If it easily sublimes and shows a disposition, at intervals, to subside at the bottom of the vessel, all is well conducted hitherto; for the moisture will first be predominant, which the sulphur can only perfectly absorb as the heat is increased for the perfect ripening of our Paradisiacal Fruit. Therefore, if it manifests a too early disposition for fixing, add more of the corrected mercury till Luna rises resplendent in her season; she will give place to the Sun in his turn. This would be the language of an adept on this occasion, only suggesting that the female quality in our prepared seed is first active, while the male is passive, and that it is afterwards passive while the male is active, such being the case in all vegetation; for every germ which is the first rudiments of a herb or tree, is predominant in moisture, and then only becomes fixed when it is fully concocted in the seed.

CHAPTER IX

Of the Further Treatment and Ripening of our Seed

This is deservedly called the Great Work of the Philosophers; and the artist having done his part hitherto, must seal up his glass hermetically, an operation which every maker of barometers knows how to perform.

The glass is then to be put into a furnace with a proper nest contrived for its reception, so as to give a continual heat from the first to the fourth degree, and to afford the artist an opportunity, from time to time, of inspecting every change which his matter assumes during the process, without danger of damping the heat and putting a stop to its perfect circulation. A heat of the first degree is sufficient at the first, for some months, in which method much time may be lost by a young practitioner, till he knows how to handle his matter from experience; but then he is not so liable to be disappointed with the bursting of his vessel or the matter vitrifying.

Thus you have arrived at the desired seed-time in our Philosophical Work, which, though it may appear in the artist's power to ripen, depends no less on the Divine blessing than the harvest, which a painful husbandman has not the presumption to expect otherwise than from God's beneficence.

There are many requisites to entitle anyone to the possession of our philosophical harvest, and the true laborers in it have sought for such persons to whom they might communicate it, by evident testimony of the senses, after which they account the confection of our Stone an easy process, manageable by women and children; but without such a communication, there is a necessity that those who would undertake it are endowed by Nature with an ingenious mind, patient to observe and accurate to investigate her ordinary appearances which, from their commonness, are less noticed than such phenomena as are more curious though of less importance; yet these for the most part employ the precious time of those egregious triflers, the modern virtuosi. These smatterers in discovery of a shell or butterfly differently streaked from those of the same kind: and all the while water, air, earth, fire, with their continual changes and resolutions into one another, by the medium of our atmosphere, through the efficacy of the central and solar heat, are unstudied by these would-be philosophers; so that a sensible rustic has more real knowledge, in this respect, than a collector of natural rarities, and makes a much wiser use of the experiences he has acquired.

CHAPTER X

Of the Further Process to the Ripening of our Noble Seed

Supposing such dispositions in the artist as have been previously laid down, and the work well performed hitherto, for his direction herein we shall describe the changes which our subject undergoes during the second part of the process, commonly called the Great Work of the Philosophers.

Our vessel being warily heated at the first for fear of its cracking, an ebullition of the contained matter is brought on, so that the moisture is alternately circulated in white fumes above, and condensed below, which may continue for a month or two, nay longer, increasing the heat gradually to another degree, as your matter discovers a disposition for fixing, by the vapor continuing at longer intervals condensed, and rising in a lesser quantity, of an ash color, or other dark shades, which it will assume as a medium to perfect blackness, the first desirable stage in our harvest. Other colors may be exhibited in this part of the work without danger, if they pass transiently; but if a faint redness, like that of the corn poppy, continues, the matter is in danger of vitrifying, either from an impatient urging of the fire, or the moisture not being sufficiently predominant. An ingenious artist can remedy this by opening his vessel and adding more of the corrected mercury, sealing it up as before; but a novice would do much better to prevent it by governing his fire according to the appearances of his matter, with judgment and patience, increasing it if the moisture manifests its predominancy too long, and slacking if the dry prevails, till such time as the vapors become dark; and after they have continued for some time at rest, a pellicle or film on the matter shows its disposition for fixing, retaining the vapor captive for some time, till it breaks through at different places on its surface (much like the bituminous substance of coal in a soldering fire), with darker clouds, but quickly dissipated, and growing less in quantity, till the whole substance resembles molten pitch, or the aforesaid bituminous substance, bubbling less and less, resting in one entire black substance at the bottom of your glass. This is called the blackness of black, the head of the crow, etc., and is esteemed a desirable stage in our philosophical generation, being the perfect putrefaction of our seed, which will ere long show its vital principle by a glorious manifestation of Seminal Virtue.

CHAPTER XI
A Further Description of the Process

When the putrefaction of our seed has been thus completed, the fire may be increased till glorious colors appear, which the Sons of Art have called Cauda Pavonis, or the Peacock's Tail. These colors come and go, as heat is administered approaching to the third degree, till all is of a beautiful green, and as it ripens assumes a perfect whiteness, which is the White Tincture, transmuting the inferior metals into silver, and very powerful as a medicine. But as the artist well knows it is capable of a higher concoction, he goes on increasing his fire till it assumes a yellow, then an orange or citron color; and then boldly gives a heat of the fourth degree, till it acquires a redness like blood taken from a sound person, which is a manifest sign of its thorough concoction and fitness for the uses intended.

CHAPTER XII
Of the Stone and its Uses

Having thus completed the operation, let the vessel cool, and on opening it you will perceive your matter to be fixed into a ponderous mass, thoroughly of a scarlet color, which is easily reducible to powder by scraping, or otherwise, and in being heated in the fire flows like wax, without smoking, flaming, or loss of substance, returning when cold to its former fixity, heavier than gold, bulk for bulk, yet easy to be dissolved in any liquid, in which a few grains being taken its operation most wonderfully pervades the human body, to the extirpation of all disorders, prolonging life by its use to its utmost period; and hence it has obtained the appellation of "Panacea,"or a Universal Remedy. Therefore, be thankful to the Most High for the possession of such an inestimable jewel, and account the possession of it not as the result of your own ingenuity, but a gift bestowed, of God's mere bounty, for the relief of human infirmities, in which your neighbor ought to share jointly with you, without any grudging or sinister views, according to the charge delivered to the Apostles: Freely have you received, freely communicate, remembering at the same time not to cast your pearls before swine; in a word, to withhold the manifestations of Nature you are enabled to exhibit, by the possession of our Stone, from the vicious and unworthy.

CHAPTER XIII
Of the Transmutation

It is much to be lamented that the seekers of natural knowledge in this art propose, principally, the Science of Transmutation as their ultimate view, and overlooking the chief excellency of our Stone as a medicine.

Notwithstanding this groveling spirit, we shall commit the issue to His Providence, and declare the Transmutation (*which, indeed, the philosophers do*) openly, after which we shall describe the further circulation of our Stone for an increase of its virtues, and then make an end of our treatise.

When the artist would transmute any metal- for instance, lead- let a quantity be melted in a clean crucible, to which let a few grains of gold in filings be cast; and when the whole is melted, let him have in readiness a little of the powder, which will easily scrape off from his "stone," the quantity inconsiderable, and cast it on the metal while in fusion.

Immediately there will arise a thick fume, which carries off with it the impurities contained in the lead, with a crackling noise, and leaves the substance of the lead transmuted into most pure gold, without any kind of sophistication; the small quantity of gold added, previous to projection, serves only as a medium to facilitate the transmutation, and the quantity of your tincture is best ascertained by experience, as its virtue in proportioned to the number of circulations you have given after the first has been completed.

For instance: when you have finished the stone, dissolve it in our mercury again, wherein you have previously dissolved a few grains of pure gold. This operation is done without trouble, both substances readily liquefying. Put it into your vessel, as before, and go through the process. There is no danger in the management, but breaking your vessel; and every time it is thus treated its virtues are increased, in a ratio of ten to one hundred, a thousand, ten thousand, etc., both in medicinal and transmuting qualities; so that a small quantity may suffice for the purposes of an artist during the remaining term of his life.